# Pulpit in the p shed

Poetry, verse and song by

Bob Flowerdew

# Contents

My dear Johnny
Love is a drug
Kids kitsch
MCP
Psycho.
Down and Out
Remedial therapy
Filthy Lucre
Poor Bawdrons
Good life song
Endgame
Will

## Daisy chain

Mistaking an albatross for a garland of flowers I
hung it around my neck,
imagining their scent and form would life and
soul bedeck.
Instead it robbed me of my hours and drove me
mad with flies.
But rather than admit mistake I still listen to it's
lies...

# The fall

I watch Autumn falling;
wan mellow days drift by,
turning trees reflecting
sun setting from the sky.

Dropping leaves tracing
your face upon the air,
departing and a leaving
boughs and twigs so bare.

Grasses khaki dying,
bare soil cold and dank.
Summer's life expiring
our sun, too soon, it sank.

Bitter gales come raping
pillaging our land, and
wild life flees so fleeting;
their hour-glass out of sand.

Hard times rudely on us
cold winds harshly cry,
for long, too long, now drabness;
there'll be no more warm skies.

For Winter rules; a cruel tide,
it's burdens know no rest.
Oh Spring you have too long to hide
until our life's re-blessed.

## Japanese vines

haiku go-by or  hi, coo-coo, bye

 With more gravitas though-


Two vines,
dancing to the sun,
touch,
entwine,
draw close
and then grow on...

# Neither meat nor meet

a refutation of Tennessee William's poem on the
Orange tree in Night of the Iguana, and a
question for over-righteous vegetarians

Here in this peaceful resting place,
too often murder does make haste;
within these walls of living green
do pass dark deeds, always unseen.

How cruel it is that with each pass
the placid man can slaughter grass;
tender heart so untoward,
to the crying of that sward.

When the weeding chores are done
then more short lives fade with the sun;
their withered corpses soon bereft
of meaning in a seed-less death.

Pausing, wiping sweat from brow,
whilst sawing branch and hacking bough,
tears forth each limb on earth to lie;
how hears he not their dying cry?

Not calmly does that Orange tree
give up its life, so cease to be,
without that cry, without that prayer,
without our hearing its despair.

Perchance it's not the carnivore
if sin the most who slay the more.
So easy 'tis to kill that spark
which lives unseen within the bark.

# In the midst of death we are in life

originally sung / chanted to Old Hundredth

Toil of our fathers still makes our crops grow,
soil and the garden their blood, sweat and fears.
The air we inhale, once the breath of heroes,
by the sea re-distilled from a myriad tears.

From ashes to ashes, through earth and rebirth,
like a river we wind ever on to that sea.
Cot till corruption, a Life, it's own worth.
Each drop not a tear but a jewel it can be.

From dust we have come and to dust we shall
go,
such a blossoming briefly, time's precious
flower.
Between changing banks same river does flow,
and our sun keeps arising always her due hour.

While we search out a reason, a meaning, a
cause,
for some the sun's setting, their last day on
Earth.
We're missing the triumph, for death's but a
pause,
with each day breaking blessing new birth.

# Fame

"My name is Ozymandius" said, oh what was his
name?
and so and so's 'David' just plays that same
sweet game.
The search for immortality; nay fortune, power
but Fame,
bedevils poor humanity who take pleasure in
such pain.

Genius may be the seed within, hard work will
go unread,
And when craft becomes the man he soon
becomes misled.
Publicity, a great life needs, your ego must be
bled,
remember, if you would succeed, it's easier
when you're dead.

## old ploughs

Forever done it's days of carving clay;
left sodden mould to moulder in,
worn plough's discarded upon the ley.

Old ploughs rusting amongst nettles
behind the old barn where within
dwells new plough; all gleaming metal.

New plough now dispatches sward.
Slices with coulter, share and tie,
never pausing, thrusting, always onward.

How deftly new plough turns virgin earth;
spreads shining smooth skinned thigh,
dark forearms, curving breasts of turf.

Beneath that skin of sea-gulled surf;
forgotten, rotten, long gone to ground,
lie yet older ploughs of wooden birth.

New plough, unaware while cleaving clod,
escapes numbering sun's course around,
knows not but all so soon interred in sod.

For sun up, sun down, each day a space,
a chance to be, to strive, to race,
yet all too soon – it is another's place.

## Plough on

Though field be great or furrow long,
plough well plough on for days soon gone,
once good job done fair rest you'll find.
The soil may stick and roots may bind,
endure those stones, hold fast your way;
wish not for end; waits there; decay.

## Mendacious memory

A fake, a fraud, a forgery,
deceives, distorts, duplicity.
Not truth nor true veracity,
the subtlest lies our memories.

# Prehistoric schizophrenic Janus

Koestler postulated split personality
twixt old and cerebral overlay.
Perchance for the mere possibility
we were worms with a head for each way.

My toe tapping in time to music
with pen writing attuned to mind.
Half in front with eyes and hands
And half behind, through toes and glands.

# Evanescent femininity

Once I saw you on an escalator
serenely gliding beyond my cry,
and just when I'd turned a corner,
thought I caught a glimpse your eye.

I watch you pass by on a train,
just waiting for a bus,
hurrying to see a game,
amongst the crowd soon lost.

Sometime you're in a lover's glance
too brief to ever surely know,
or there, a fleeting shot askance,
up on another's picture show.

Alluring phantom, you're seen, to flee,
escaping my reality.
Or is it I, the ghost to thee?
Evanescent femininity.

# Lunacy

Clawing skyward Macbeth's new dagger
soaring mighty silver phallus
epitome of Man's desire
extra terrestrial space age palace.
While legions starve upon the ground
above their heads glides round around
blasphemous waste, the ultimate irony
a satellite of scrap ironmongery
inane statue to inhumanity
claimed as triumph, mere insanity.

## Legacy

How bare a forest without trees
how quiet a meadow without bees
how flat the city with no towers
how strange the ground that bears no flowers.
The soil is grey, the soil is dry
above it now no bird does fly
across the earth a harsh wind blows
upon it's face no plant does grow.
Mankind's age has come and gone,
amongst their 'gifts' the nuclear bomb.

## to a fallen star

Did you try to live a story
turn the World into your dream?
Built up of fancied glories
was it not as you had seen?

The critics turned you bitter
their wit to put you down;
seditious words and letters
made your hero seem the clown.

But you can have the last laugh
if you really are that strong.
The best revenge that one can craft,
live well, live well, live long!

## Present and correct sir

Presentient present,
prescient presence,
impassioned incessant,
imprisoned in sentence.

## Rhyme no reason

Rich rhymes with switch,
with pitch, hitch, and ditch,
with snitch, kitsch and witch
and unfortunately, bitch.

Poor rhymes with raw,
gore, sore and tore,
war, whore and bore,
and comically, law.

## Ici et maintenant

Here, a different place before,
again another follows.

Now, naught but yesterdays
always searching for tomorrows.

Life, too brief a memory
of laughter, pain and sorrows.

Time is that holy gift,
like love, we only borrow.

## Old Soho

Standing on a city corner,
traffic lights glaring red.
'French Massage', 'Swedish Sauna'.
'Breasts and Buttocks', 'Must Be Read'.
Come cultivate a kinky fetish;
rubber knickers, black silk truss.
Forbidden, ever hidden wish;
furtive matters, but little fuss.
'Live Girl Show', 'Stripping Nightly',
'Transvestites', a screaming queen.
Jehovah's Witness protesting mightily;
Armageddon will soon be seen.
Standing on a city corner,
traffic lights now gone green.

# Bang, Bang, Bang your drum.

(variation on traditional)

Bang, Bang, Bang your drum. Bang, Bang, Bang
your drum.
Bang, Bang, Bang your drum.
Bang it loud. Bang it long. We'll not go to war.

Bang, Bang, Bang your drum. Bang, Bang, Bang
your drum.
Bang, Bang, Bang your drum.
Take our brave. Take our young. We'll not go to
war.

Bang, Bang, Bang your drum. Bang, Bang, Bang
your drum.
Bang, Bang, Bang your drum.
To make you rich will make us poor. We'll not go
to war.

Bang, Bang, Bang your drum. Bang, Bang, Bang
your drum.
Bang, Bang, Bang your drum.
Tell us lies then tell us more. We'll not go to war.

Bang, Bang, Bang your drum. Bang, Bang, Bang
your drum.
Bang, Bang, Bang your drum.

## Flash Harry

Furtive glance,
crouching stance,
quietly stalking,
old maid walking.
Alley black,
opens mac,
standing there.
Frightened stare.
Screaming, shouting.
Panic mounting,
turns and runs,
he's had his fun.
Knowing not,
not care a jot,
a damaged one
more damage done.

## Even song

Sitting here on wooden seat
wind rustling Autumn leaves
floor so cold on tender feet
trousers down below the knees,
out of tune, singing blues,
the poetry of outdoor loos.

## Sun sign

When a beam comes warmly smiling from skies
of azure blue
to cease the zephyrs sighing, it's then I dream of
you...

# Now your wooden leg is rusting

Your eyes like warm puddles of oily water
brown green the middle, streaked red the rest.
Nails bit down, toenails the shorter,
hunch back balancing flat chest.
Greasy hair covers round shoulders,
bandy, pigeon toed, knock kneed,
dandruff snowing scabby boulders
what teeth you had have gone to seed.
and now your wooden leg is rusting,
between the spots your skin is pale.
Believe me, were you this disgusting,
my love for you could still not fail.

## Get Betjeman

to sell this house she said, so in Evening
Standard property gallery I advertised her house
at the head of Mount Street, Diss, one of his
favourite country town places-

Diss- 86 mins from Liverpool St. station,
short stroll to des. res. location
17C. cottage & ancient yew
look out over Betjeman's favourite view.
With original beams & inglenook;
3 beds, 2 recep, glazed space to cook.
Small sunny garden, patio,
space to park & stained glass too.
All mod. cons in recent extension.
Squash, golf, tennis, stables nearby release
tension.
£80,000 immediately available,
fittings & furniture all on the table.

## Uncle Eric

Gardeners Question Time's long running chair,
Brian Blessed with all but the stare.
He too plays at God,
but if you give him the nod
you'll get in, so I must say he's fair.

## Wed-lock

(wed from the old English to join wood)

Too many know to use but nails,
the wiser also employ some glue,
yet stronger than a nut and bolt
are many damn good screws

## Prose-ache

I just closed the door slowly, savouring the
poignant click of the latch. A surging of nostalgia,
a deep sorrow, a dry tear-ing inside. She had
turned around to wave as the car drove away. A
smile had flashed across her face burning after
images onto my life. A smile imprinted by love,
to atone, for my sake, a clown's mask giving
happiness while the soul within suffers, silently,
and so alone.

# The child who'll never be

My days forlornly haunted by our child who'll
never be,
enduring nights so empty save for that memory;
of when we tried to kindle life, to make our two
come three.

How do you show a blind man just what it is you
see ?
So poor attempts at caring became read as
jealousy;
and distance came between us, bitter calamity.

Somehow I lost your love, your trust, joy and
glee,
your passionate embraces, our happy ecstasy;
& much the worse we lost our child who now
will never be.

So now there'll be no baby, no future will he see,
no children of his own to visit you and me,
no even-tide rejoicing grand-children on the
knee.

Oh how I miss your laugh, your touch, your joie
de vie,
our endless nights of passion, your sensuality.
I'm sorry if I caused you pain and lost our
empathy.

May you find your dream my love, my hope goes
out to thee.
You may never know the truth, the greatest loss
to me;

not just your happy presence but our child
who'll never be.

## Remember

Remember
The morning in the park,
the warm damp grass underfoot.
We were happy then.
We did not know what was to come.
Remember
Our first impulsive kiss,
how frightened we were.
We were happy then.
We did not know what was to come.
Remember
The afternoon by the sea
when it rained too soon.
We were happy then.
We did not know what was to come.
Remember
The night we parted.
How alone we felt.
We were unhappy then
for we knew what had come.
Remember
Life is but memories
Without them there is none.
Remember me
for I have memories of you
to richen the rest of my life.
I am not unhappy now.
I do not mind, whatever comes,
    -honestly I'm fine...

## love is a loan

Alone, alone, alone,
Now misery descends.
No-one, No-one, No-one,
Unhappiness is here.
She's gone. She's gone. She's gone.

## After

After you left
I made love to another
Only not making love
No more than screwing.
Like eating a meal
when not even hungry
like watching an old movie
for the eleventh time
like visiting relatives
so glad when they're gone.
A mere empty gesture,
after, you've left.

## seven years

Seven years since you said goodbye.
Seven years for love to die.
Seven years through which to cry,
and yet, that love, you did despise.

Seven years, of course you're wed,
taken to another's bed.
Why still I wait with face so red
with tears for love now so long dead?

So long ago vainly I tried
to show the love that you decried.
Seven years, unsatisfied,
I've hoped so for that love revived.

I wish that love would turn to hate,
but on it burns so still I wait.
If seven years is not too late,
from love denied, give me escape.

## Cider glasses

With more cider inside ya you'll feel good inside,
With more cider inside ya you'll be well revived,
With more cider inside ya you'll not be tongue
tied,
With more cider inside ya you're in over drive.
With more cider inside ya your bladder'll say Hi,
With more cider inside ya your brain say's good-
bye,
With more cider inside ya you'll go all pie eyed,
With more cider inside ya you'll walk with legs
tied.
With more cider inside ya you'll look for a bride,
With more cider inside ya she won't look so
wide,
With more cider inside ya her hair won't look
dyed,
With more cider inside ya her wrinkles will hide.
With more cider inside ya it's best you have lied,
With more cider inside ya you'll wish you had
died,
With more cider inside her you're best satisfied,
With more cider inside ya; that's just suicide.

# My dear Johnny

to be sung to the traditional folk tune.

I know what I'm doing
& I know who's doing it with me.
but just to be quite safe
I will wear a rubber johnny.
Chorus

Chorus
Some will say they spoil it.
Some will say they're smelly
but I say one will help you last
as long as on the telly.

Some like ones in black
some even like them funny.
I wear one 'cos it's sensible
a protective rubber johnny.
Chorus

Just in case, maybe.
deep within my wallet.
I've got two or three,
if you ever need a johnny.
Chorus

So buy a pack today
stick one in your pocket.
Just you wait you'll say
Have you met my good mate Johnny?
Chorus

# Love is a drug

-not an endorsement but "I get a hit out of you",
 may be sung to "All things bright & beautiful"

All drugs are they wonderful?
Intoxicants strong or mild.
Taken by the thimbleful
become as a little child.

From starry ey-ed acid
to sweetest Mary Jane.
Take them by the bucketful
you'll drive yourself in-sane.

That little magic mushroom.
The leaf that makes you cough
The yeasts that make the wine flow
and all that powdery stuff.

Quaff coffee in the morning
cocoa last fix at night,
the cup of tea stops yawning
a pill if you're uptight.

But the best drug is a lover,
withdrawal's pretty tough
for more than with the others
you can never have enough.

# Kids kitsch

song for a boy band

Together and together we shall forever be,
You and your sweet whispers and a very happy
me.
We'll talk of many, many things,
You as Queens and I as Kings,
Build our castles in the skies,
See through all with magic eye.
By your side I'll take your hand
to guide us through this mystic land.
Thou a Princess I a Knight,
I shall have you for my right.
For in our dreams I can never be
parted from your company.
We'll rule the world from far above
with that power of pure, true love.
oh yuck!

## MCP

Male Chauvinist Pig / Mathematically Created
Person
from 'The Brothers Karamazov' on the curve of
her neck being repeated in her ear and the turn
of her ankle.

Womankind; function divine.
Subtle curve, integrated,
extended, created,
alongside man in mind.

# Psycho.

Main song for rock opera 'Un-tended
consequences'

I'm gonna to tell of the wrong I done,
all started out with harmless fun,
I killed a man, well left him for dead,
his tongue was black and his face was red,
his jaw was slack and his eyes bulged out,
and all because he'd called ME a lout!
While all around the eyes they stared,
Watching, waiting, but I couldn't see where.

I grabbed my jacket, started to run,
thought about what had been harmless fun,
of the poor old ladies we'd frightened and
scared,
of the crimes we'd committed while everyone
glared.
How cruel I'd been, how tough and hard.
Every-things fair, no holds barred.
While all around the eyes they stared,
Watching, waiting, but I couldn't see where.

So now by myself a murder I'd done,
and I was doomed to be on the run.
I left that street and ran through the night,
while everywhere round were flashing blue
lights,
fled down an alley then under some stairs,
stayed amongst crowds and hid in a fair.
While all around the eyes they stared,
Watching, waiting, but I couldn't see where.

Cont'd.


A kindly old man gave me shelter and bed,
he asked the wrong question oh how he bled.
A pretty girl saw my face and screamed,
didn't hit her hard so it had seemed,
she too dropped down, another dead?
Her face contorted, her blouse going red.
While all around the eyes they stared,
Watching, waiting, but I couldn't see where.

I hid her quickly and ran out again
Running through the wind and rain.
I searched for shelter, couldn't find none,
couldn't stop thinking about what I'd done.
So now in this dump I find myself,
damp in the cellar, rats on the shelf,
While all around the eyes they stare,
Watching, waiting, and now I see where.

I'm writing this and I think I know why,
I had never a choice, for all we must die.
Once round my neck, twice round the beam,
hope I'm not ugly when I am seen.
The floor so distant, in my throat a lump,
all thats left me, my freedom, the jump.

## Down and Out

So now I'm homeless, what's called a 'has-been'
all over your cities I'm easily seen.
Waiting by gratings, waiting in tubes
waiting by stations, waiting in queues.
My stomach is empty my ribs are bare,
my misery's obvious but nobody cares.
My feet are roughshod, in my shoes paper bags,
my teeth are half gone, my clothes but rags.
My eyes aren't bad, my ears can be poor,
my arms are weak, and my back is sore.
My hands are clean but my lips are thin
through holes in my clothes the wind whistles
in.
My food is from bins and what I must steal
I cannot remember when last had 'a meal'.
My house a squat, it's to be pulled down
I'm just staying there until They come round.
It's not really mine but it's all I have got
complete with foul stench and rampant dry rot.
I'll be dead very soon and then you'll be glad
for it shames you to think of the life that I've
had.
You may talk of your dole and the Welfare State
but that's only for those with work who pay
rates.
For awkwards like me, those 'down and outs'
You leave only one way and that's the WAY
OUT...

# Remedial therapy

Best sung to swing or calypso

Smoking Gambling Drinking?
No, I'd rather;
make it like a sailor
when the boats in harbour.
Spending all your cache, giving up your stash
you've gotta be real rash if you want to make a
splash.

Living Loving Laughing,
Life's a gala;
with a pocket full of money
go the massage parlour.
Spending all your cache, giving up your stash
you've gotta be real rash if you want to make a
splash.

For girls get spending thrills,
oh they'll do what you will,
when you really want their honey
you just gotta give them money.
Spending all your cache, giving up your stash
you've gotta be real rash if you want to make a
splash.

You wanna hear them hollah
Just throw around your dollar,
And to make them all a quiver;
pour champagne out in a river.
Spending all your cache, giving up your stash

you've gotta be real rash if you want to make a splash.

# Filthy Lucre

may be sung to Glory Hallelujah or Onward
Christian soldiers

A paradise was made this Earth, the writings on
the wall.
Realise it now for what it's worth, it was given to
us all.
So keep your filthy lucre for there's no New
Land to find.
We all will have no future; we need a change of
mind.

Sweet rivers now polluted, the naked rocks been
hewn.
Our countryside's commuted, by-products o'er
all strewn.
So keep your filthy lucre for there's no New
Land to find.
We all will have no future without that change of
mind.

Forests now a thicket, our woodlands nearly
bare.
Beauty spot they take it, to put a gift shop there.
So keep your filthy lucre for there's no New
Land to find.
We all will have no future unless we change
their mind.

Moors and marshes crying, hedgerows torn,
burned.
Wild lives all expiring, you leave no stone
unturned.

So keep your filthy lucre for there's no New
Land to find.
We all will have no future unless we change your
mind.

Cities turned malignant, wastelands are their
spawn.
Smogs and urban sprawl obscure the budding
dawn.
So keep your filthy lucre for there's no New
Land to find.
We all will have no future unless we change our
minds.

A paradise was made this Earth, the writings on
the wall.
Realise it now for what it's worth, it was given to
us all.
So keep your filthy lucre for there's no New
Land to find.
There's coming a great future if we do but
change our mind.

## Poor Bawdrons

Traditional Cameronian Cat, with some minor alterations and additions, top and tail, to be sung.

A holiday, no, a holy day, culmination of the week.
Six days meant for labour, the seventh thou must keep.

Once a zealous priests' house-cat went forth to catch her prey
And brought a mouse into the house upon his Sabbath day.
The minister offended with such an act profane, laid down his book, the cat he took and bound her with a chain.

"Though vile malicious creature, thou murderer" said he,
"Oh do you think to fetch to hell my holy wife and me?"
"But be thou well assured that blood for blood shall pay;
for taking of wee mousey's life upon my Sabbath day."

Then he dropped down upon his knees, so fervently he prayed,
that the great sin the cat had done, might not on him be laid.

The whole house was assembled and made to doff their hats.
God's word it was expounded, then judged to damn the cat.

So forth to execution poor Bawdrons she was drawn,
upon a tree they'd hang her high, and then they'd sing a psalm.
But when he pulled upon the rope, the great tree it did fall.
Poor Bawdrons escaped the crush that killed the family all.

A holiday, no a holy day, culmination of the week.
Six days meant for labour. The seventh thou should keep.

# Good life song

The real good life is a husband and wife,
with their kids all round their pot.
Their strength derived from the food inside;
all grown on their backyard plot.
No toxic wastes, no artificial tastes,
will cheat their health away;
for nutritious food's the righteous road
it's grow your own; don't pay.

For factory food's the devil's load;
take-outs cost dear one day.
A moment on your lips, lifetime on your hips,
be lucky to escape to old age.
The food you eat IS your body's meat!
Don't cheat, and don't delay.
As it's no joke; a tumour or a stroke;
may be just one bite away.

So forget the gym if your garden you trim
you'll soon work off that lard.
Stop big talk, take up your fork;
it'll make your body hard.
Go feed your soil with compost, and toil
to keep the weeds at bay,
the bugs to pick, the blights we trick
we need no chemical sprays.

Eat organic foods, follow good codes;
to grow, to read, to pray.
Man's got the lot who tends his plot;
God's work to do each day.

## End-game

There is a debt we all must pay;
May be tomorrow, perhaps today.
Run or hide or play or pray;
grim reaper's scythe you cannot stay.

# Will

or 'the human condition', one of the first

Will you remember me ?
Will I exist ?
What will the future be ?
Will I be missed ?
Will I be slandered ?
Will I be praised ?
If I were martyred
would a statue be raised ?
Will I be worshipped ?
Will I be cussed ?
Will I be forgotten
when I am dust?


...and on more assertive/miserable days

So if I'm not worshipped
then let me be cuss'd
that I'm not forgotten
now I am dust.

Printed in Great Britain
by Amazon